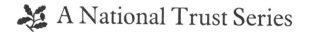 A National Trust Series

Fireships Away!

THE INSIDE STORY OF
THE SPANISH ARMADA

Harry T Sutton

BATSFORD–HERITAGE BOOKS

Illustrations: Chapters 1 and 2, Ron Stenberg; Chapter 2,
Vivian Turner; Chapter 3, Moira Clinch

Contents

1 On Beacon Hill

Susan Brad was 'marking' for her brother at archery practice.

'Gone!' she called, as the arrow flew high over the target. Her brother strung another arrow to his bow and took aim.

'Wide!' his sister called, as the arrow missed again. But then, when the boy's bow flexed a third time, she ran to the target and stood staring at it in amazement.

'You have split the peg, Dick!' she exclaimed. 'It is split right down the middle!'

In a moment her brother was by her side, looking delightedly at the peg which held the cloth target in place. . . Sure enough, the last arrow had hit it fair and square – the wooden peg was neatly split in half. It was the best possible shot and one which every archer was proud to achieve.

'Leave it Susan,' Dick told his sister as he picked up the arrows which had gone wide. 'Father will want to see this!'

It was a fine July day in the year 1588. The two children were playing at the old archery butts on Fairlight Down, near their home by the sea. The butts, earth banks to which targets were fixed, had been built 40 years before, when Henry the Eighth was king. There was a threat of invasion from France then and everybody, even boys of seven and eight, had to practise archery by law. Now there was another invasion threat, this time from Spain; and once again the people of England were preparing for war.

Elizabeth the First was Queen of England and the ways of fighting wars had changed. Soldiers were now armed with muskets and the longbow was out of date.

'Archers cannot match musketeers,' people said. But Dick's father was not so sure. He was a watchman at the beacons on Fairlight Down, looking out for enemy ships, and he knew England's danger only too well.

'You keep a-practising, my lad,' he told Dick. 'If that there Spanish Armada do come this way, us'll need muskets *and* bows and arrows too, I reckon!'

And Susan had gone with her brother once or twice a week for Dick to practise. Now, for the first time, he had shot the arrow which was every archer's delight. He had split the peg!

'Let's go and ask father to come and see it,' she suggested. And the children started off across the Downs to where their father was on watch.

The villagers of Fairlight used the Downs for many things. It was common land where they could graze their cattle and sheep; the village stocks were there into which people were locked to serve their punishments in public disgrace; fairs and markets were held there; and on warm summer days lovers strolled across its sheep-cropped grass whilst the old folk sat and gazed out to sea, remembering the days when they were young.

But on this particular summer day, when Dick practised his archery, the Downs had a much more important part to play. Not far from the church, at the highest point of the Downs,

three wooden towers with iron braziers on top, stood tall against the skyline. They were beacons set up to give warning of enemy ships and it was to the watchman's hut that Dick and Susan now came, to tell their father about the arrow which had split the peg.

Will Hobben, a neighbour in Fairlight, was the other watchman that day and when Dick told the story of the arrow, he teased the boy in a friendly way.

'Are you sure that there peg didn't split of its own accord?' he asked him, a twinkle in his eye. 'Broke in half naturally-like, on account of being fried by the sun?'

'No, Mister Hobben,' said Dick, indignantly. ''Twas my arrow that split it right enough, weren't it Sue?' And he looked to his sister for her support.

But Susan was not listening. From where they stood by the

beacons, there was a fine view in all directions and now, shading her eyes, Susan pointed along the coast to the west.

'Look, father,' she said. 'Smoke is coming from that hill!' And following her gaze, John Brad saw it too.

''Tis on Cooden Down,' he exclaimed. 'One of the beacons is lit and that means the Armada is in sight!'

He turned to Will Hobben.

'We cannot light our beacons until Squire Ashburnham gives the order,' he said. 'You go off and tell him, Will, and I'll stay on watch.'

Broomham, the big country house where Squire Ashburnham lived, was two and a half miles away and Will Dobben did not own a horse. He would have to run all the way and, standing by their father, the children watched him as he started off across the Downs.

'Mister Hobben can run fast, can't he father,' said Susan, admiringly. But then, suddenly, they saw him fall. He tried to get up but could not.

'He must be hurt,' exclaimed John Brad and, with the children following, he went across to where Will was lying on the ground, his face twisted in pain.

'Broke my blessed ankle I reckon,' he said with a groan, as they came up to him. 'Caught my foot in a rabbit scrape.'

'Somehow the Squire must be told though,' said John Brad.

'And you'll never be able to go now, Will. Nor can I leave the hut.' Then he turned to Dick.

'You must run there, son!' he told him. 'You know the way to Broomham, don't you?'

Dick's heart pounded with excitement.

'Yes, father, of course I do,' he replied.

'Then off you go, lad. Tell the Squire that Cooden Down beacon is lit and will he please come here directly.' Then he looked seriously at his son. 'Can you remember that Dick?' he asked him. 'No mistakes now!'

'Yes, father,' said Dick, and he repeated the message word for word.

'Good,' said his father. 'And you must not fail to get there, lad. 'Tis news of the Spanish Armada. You'll never carry a more important message for England in your life!'

'Don't worry, father,' said Dick. 'I'll not fail.'

Fairlight Down was so high that the way to Broomham was nearly all downhill. But even so, those two and a half miles were the longest Dick had ever run. He was ten years old and used to taking messages from place to place. 'Just run up to the mill for me, Dick', his mother would say. And he would run all the way, uphill too, from their cottage to Fairlight mill. But that was only to get flour for his mother to make bread.

The message he carried now, as he raced across fields and through woods, was far more important than that.

'What if I fall, like Will Hobben?' he asked himself. 'The Armada might come and land its army without our soldiers

being warned!'

He knew what would happen if the Spaniards did land for his father and mother had often talked about it round the fire on winter nights.

'They'll kill us all, sure as fate', his mother had said. 'Women and children too, for them Spaineys are a cruel lot from all I've heard!' His father, too, said they were cruel people who would burn houses and steal all the food, if ever they got ashore in England.

'I must get to Broomham, I *must*,' Dick told himself. And he ran even faster until his lungs seemed ready to burst.

Adam Ashburnham was in the great hall at Broomham when Dick arrived. At first the boy was so out of breath that he could not make himself understood.

'Sit down for a moment, lad,' said the Squire, kindly. 'You're John Brad's boy, are you not?' And when Dick nodded, the Squire suddenly understood. 'He is watchman at the beacons this week, isn't he?' he asked.

'Yes, sir,' said Dick, recovering his breath. 'He sent me to tell you that Cooden Down beacon is lit and will you please come directly.'

Squire Ashburnham wasted no time.

Round the walls of the big dining hall were hung suits of armour, pikes, helmets, swords and lances. Ashburnhams of the past had used them in wars of long ago and they were now only hung as decorations. But the Squire took down one of the swords and fastening the sword-belt round his waist he ran quickly out of the hall, telling Dick to follow.

'Giles, Giles!' he shouted, as they came to the stables at the back of the house, and when his groom appeared he told him:

'Saddle Molly for me, Giles, I'm wanted up at Fairlight Down!' and when the man brought the big mare from its stable, the Squire helped him to tighten the girths.

'Can I come, sir?' asked Dick, as the Squire mounted his horse.

'Yes, lad. You have done your duty to the Queen this day,' said the Squire. 'You deserve a ride for you must be tired after such a long run.'

He nodded to the groom.

'Help the boy up, Giles,' he told him. Then as Dick settled himself behind the Squire on the big hunter's broad back, Adam Ashburnham called back to him:

'Hold on tight now,' and he put the mare straight into a gallop.

At the beacons on the Downs, John Brad had just managed to get his injured neighbour back to the watchmen's hut when Squire Ashburnham galloped up with young Dick, grinning broadly, riding behind.

'Is it Cooden Down then, John?' the Squire asked. And he shaded his eyes the better to see the distant hill beyond which the evening sun was already beginning to set.

'Aye, sir, it has been lit for nearly an hour now,' replied John. The Squire looked out to sea, then to the east where the coast of Kent snaked away beyond the little harbour of Rye,

to the point of Dungeness and to the cliffs of Dover beyond.

'No ships in sight yet,' he said. 'Up with you then, John, and set fire to number one beacon.'

'Everything is ready, sir,' said John. Then taking his flint and tinder box, he quickly struck a flame. A torch made of brushwood soaked in pitch stood ready and soon this was well alight. Carrying the burning torch above his head, John Brad now climbed the ladder to one of the beacons. In a moment, the pitch-soaked wood in the big iron fire-basket was burning and black smoke began to rise in the still evening air.

'The Kent watchers will see that all right,' he said, as flames began to blaze from the top.

'Aye,' said Adam Ashburnham. 'And within the hour, ten thousand soldiers will be ready to march!' Then he glanced down at Dick, standing beside his sister, watching the flames from the tall beacon.

'Your young lad did well, John Brad,' he said. 'We have wasted no time.'

Even as he spoke, villagers from Fairlight were coming, running across the Downs. Some carried old swords, others held pitchforks and hoes. One old woman was waving a frying pan as she hurried up the hill. Thomas Swann, the Rector of Fairlight church, came puffing and blowing along with the rest.

'Are they in sight, Adam?' he asked the Squire.

'Not yet, Rector,' replied the Squire. 'But they can't be far away.'

'Then I shall stay here until they come,' declared the old parson. And he settled himself comfortably on the grass beside the watch hut from where there was a clear view over the sea.

'If the Spaniards do try to land, I want to be there to see them sent running back to Spain!' he said.

Dick and Susan hardly slept that night. Dawn is early in July but even before the sun was up, they were out of bed and looking out of their cottage window to the beacons on the hill above.

'All three are lit!' exclaimed Susan, excitedly.

'They must be here!' said Dick. 'The Armada must be here!'

Even as they spoke, they heard the clatter of hooves in the lane outside and a troop of horsemen dashed by, their burnished steel helmets and breastplates glinting in the dawn light. They were splendidly dressed and their horses were the finest the children had ever seen.

'They must be officers!' whispered Dick, in wonder.

Then, soon after the horsemen had passed, there was the sound of drums and trumpets in the distance and the children, still in their nightshirts, ran down to the gate and looked along the lane. Coming towards them, flags flying and muskets over their shoulders, a long column of soldiers was marching up the hill. But before they could see them pass, the children's mother called them indoors.

'Your father did not come home last night,' she told them. 'He must have stayed on watch and he will need some food

and drink. Get dressed now both of you and then you can take it to him.'

Not stopping to wash or brush their hair, Dick and Susan quickly dressed and only minutes later they were in the kitchen ready to go. Mrs Brad gave them bread and cheese for their father and food for themselves.

'If there is danger and your father sends you home, you do as he says, mind,' she warned them.

Then the two children were off, running as hard as they could go, towards the Downs and the beacons on the hill.

The sight they saw when they reached the top, took their breath away. Out to sea, as far as the eye could see, there were ships. Hundreds of ships it seemed, row upon row, line after line. Great galleons with high prows and sterns, bristling with guns. Smaller warships, their decks lined with soldiers;

converted merchantships with guns mounted where cargo was usually placed; supply ships, pinnaces – sailing boats carried aboard the ships – and even rowing boats, busily moving around and between the fleets.

They sat in a sea, calm as a mirror. Not a whiff of breeze ruffled its smoothness and the sails on that forest of masts hung slack. For the great Spanish Armada was becalmed!

'But where are *our* ships?' Susan asked her father as he joined them on the clifftop.

'Over yonder,' he told her, pointing to other ships, also becalmed, which lay apart from the Spanish fleet, to the west.

'But they look so small,' said Dick, anxiously. 'Is that all we've got, to fight these great galleons?'

'Aye,' said his father. 'But Francis Drake is over yonder, boy. And Hawkins, Frobisher and Howard too. That makes them *big* ships, lad, you'll see!'

All that day the Armada and the English fleet lay becalmed off Fairlight. Along the clifftops, from Hastings to Dungeness, and along all the beaches between, guns were mounted pointing out to sea, and soldiers waited, ready. But not a shot was fired that day. Helpless without a breeze to fill their sails, the ships sat silent. Standing with their father, the villagers all around, watching from the clifftop, it did not seem possible that aboard those peaceful ships were ten thousand men, armed with guns and swords, come to conquer England for the King of Spain.

But then, as evening came, a wind blew up from the west and the ships of both fleets gradually began to move. As darkness fell they were still passing Fairlight Downs and the lights on their decks could be seen, disappearing into the distance – eastwards to where the Duke of Parma waited with fifty thousand men, ready for the invasion. The danger for England was still to come.

The next day was Sunday and with their mother, Dick and Susan went to Fairlight church to pray for victory. Adam Ashburnham was in the Squire's pew with his family and they too joined in the victory prayer. 'Oh Lord defend us from our enemies and send us victory by the grace of Our Lord Jesus

Christ . . .' the parson prayed from his pulpit. And all the congregation said 'Amen', remembering as they prayed that great army of ships which only yesterday had lain, so menacingly quiet and so dangerously close.

'Amen,' they all said. 'Amen.'

Out at sea, the same Sunday morning, a very different group of men sat around a table in the cabin of the *Ark Royal,* the flagship of the English fleet. At anchor near the French coast within sight of the Great Armada fleet, Charles Howard the Lord Admiral, with Drake, Frobisher, Hawkins and Seymour, were discussing their next move.

'By anchoring off Calais,' said Drake, 'the Spanish fleet has played into our hands!'

'The Duke of Parma, with his invasion army, is but a few miles along the coast at Dunkirk,' the Lord Admiral reminded

him. 'Lying at Calais, the Armada is between us and Parma's invasion fleet and can keep us away. For that purpose the Armada is well placed!'

'We must move them,' declared Hawkins. 'We must send them packing, and for that we need fireships!'

'Yesterday I sent to Dover for fishing smacks,' Lord Howard told him. 'Tomorrow they will be here and then we can make fireships of them.'

'But tomorrow will be too late, My Lord,' objected Francis Drake. 'Tonight is the time for fireships, for at midnight there will be a flood tide which will flow at four knots where we lie, directly towards Calais.'

'Aye, My Lord,' agreed Hawkins. 'And if the wind stays in the west, fireships could be in amongst them before their lookouts could raise an alarm.'

'We shall have to burn some of our ships,' declared Frobisher, 'then we can attack tonight.'

The men thought about this for a moment. No seaman wants to see a good ship destroyed, especially by fire. But there seemed no other way.

Francis Drake spoke first.

'I will give my ship *Thomas* to the venture,' he said, 'It is of 200 tons and can carry a fine load of fireworks!'

'And I will give the *Hope*,' said Hawkins, 'for she is well named for the enterprise!'

And so it was decided. Eight small ships were chosen, to be under the orders of Captain John Young, an old and experienced sea captain from the west country, and all that Sunday they were prepared for their last, fiery voyage. Barrels of pitch were placed in their holds; their decks were piled with firewood; their guns were loaded so that they would go off when reached by fire; as much gunpowder as could be spared was rammed into casks which would explode and scatter burning debris far and wide. The eight ships were made into torpedoes of a very deadly kind.

Captain John Young had worked hard preparing his ship, the *Bear Yonge*, and now the time had come to set sail. It was midnight and the flood tide was pulling the heavily laden ship taut from its anchor. Looking across the moonlit sea that separated the line of fireships from the Armada fleet, the Captain made a quick calculation.

'Four to five knots of current,' he told himself, 'and this breeze should give us another six. Say ten knots allowing for sails to fill. A mile to cover. That means we should be in amongst them in five or six minutes from start.'

He turned to the mate.

'Be prepared to light all fuses directly I give the word, Mister Mate,' he told him. 'And that will be almost as soon as we are under way.'

'Aye aye, sir,' said the mate.

Captain Young looked round the familiar lines of his ship. She belonged to him and although she was small, less than 200 tons, she had given good service in her time. When the Admiral asked for volunteers to give their ships he had immediately offered the *Bear Yonge*. But it seemed a shame, nevertheless, to burn such a faithful old friend.

'Eight bells, Captain,' he heard the mate call from the poopdeck.

'Thank you, Mister Mate,' he replied. Then taking his lantern, he opened the shutter and signalled to the other waiting ships. One by one he saw their answering lights. Then, dripping anchor ropes tautened round turning capstans, sails were unfurled, and the eight ships began to move. The fireships were away.

Captain Young judged the moment for lighting fuses exactly right. Within two minutes of setting sail a red glow started and slowly grew amidships in the *Bear Yonge*. Seconds later the other seven ships were afire.

'Steady as she goes', Young called to the man at the wheel. Then, as flames began to blaze high from the foreparts of the ship, he gave the order:

'Come aft all hands'.

Quickly the small volunteer crew, four deckhands with himself and the mate, gathered on the poop. Young glanced at the dinghy towing behind in the ship's wake. It was their only means of escape.

The flames were catching the sails now as they saw the tall hulls of the Armada ships dead ahead. Part of the game was to steer the blazing ship for as long as possible, for this would make sure that one enemy ship at least would feel the heat of the flames. But there was little time left now before the fires found the gunpowder casks down below.

'Abandon ship!' he ordered at last, and they were so close that the frightened lookout on one Spanish ship heard the words. Then, his men going first, Captain Young made his escape.

The men had hardly unshipped the oars and begun to row when one of the other fireships, it looked like the *Hope*, blew up with a roar. A blazing rain of shattered timbers showered over the enemy fleet. The guns of another fireship, overheated by the flames, discharged in a ragged broadside and the sea was red with fire for a mile around.

Anchored close inshore, more than a hundred ships in packed rows, the Armada was helpless before the relentless fireships. There was only one thing for them to do. There was no time to raise their anchors; 'cut cables' was the order which now ran round the Spanish fleet. And as the fireships drifted in amongst them, the proud Armada ships hurriedly hoisted sail and fled. There were collisions; one great ship was driven ashore, to be wrecked and abandoned; others, their rigging on fire, drifted helplessly as their crews did their best to put out the flames.

But the worst was not yet over for the Spanish Armada. As daylight came, revealing the galleons scattered over ten square miles of sea, the English fleet closed in. For many hours there was the sound of gunfire, heard by the Duke of Parma's invasion army, left far behind now as the Armada tried to escape from the English guns. The gunfire grew fainter in the distance. Then there was silence.

For several days there was no news. The beacons on Fairlight Down were no longer lit for the immediate danger had passed. But the iron braziers were filled again with pitch, ready to be lit should the Armada turn in its tracks and re-enter the Channel from the east. For the invasion army was still at Dunkirk and although there had been 'a victory at Calais where the Armada had last been seen in full flight, there had been no news of it since.

Every day, Dick and Susan went with their father to the beacon hut to keep watch with him, for the sight of that great fleet so recently lying becalmed was still fresh in their minds.

'If they do come back,' Squire Ashburnham had said, 'it will mean that our ships have been sunk, for only if they can defeat Drake and Hawkins will the Spaniards dare to try their luck again.'

But there was no news of victory, nor of defeat. And on the hilltop at Fairlight, as along all the coasts of England, the watch was still kept day and night – just in case.

Then, one day, news did come. Susan was with her brother on the Downs, marking for him again as he practised at the archery butts, when they heard a gun firing, then they heard several more. Running to the beacons, they asked their father what it could mean. But he knew no more than they.

'It sounds like a gun salute,' he told them. 'It is coming from Rye Harbour and perhaps some important Lord has just landed there and the guns are being fired in his honour.'

Then in the distance they heard church bells.

'It is not Sunday,' said Susan, 'so what can *that* mean?'

But they were soon to know. Up the hill from Guestling there came a horseman, riding hard their way. It was the Squire and they saw him dismount and run into Church House where the Rector lived. Minutes later, the bell in Fairlight church began to sound, then the bell at Guestling church was heard as well.

''Tis a victory!' the Squire shouted, as he now rode up to the beacons. 'A ship has sailed into Rye with news of the Armada's defeat. The Spaniards are scattered and what is left of them are on their way to Scotland!'

'We haven't got a cannon up here Squire, but can we fire our muskets to mark the victory?' asked Dick's father.

'Aye, John,' said the Squire, with a laugh. 'And I'll fire one of them myself too.' And for a time the hilltop at Fairlight resounded with the bangs of the watchmen's guns, fired not in anger, but in celebration.

Dick Brad picked up his bow and fitted an arrow.

'That's for the Duke of Parma!' he shouted, and the arrow sped away, high over the Downs to the east where the Spanish fleet had sailed away.

Then he fitted another arrow to the bow and this time he

aimed it to the west.

'That's for the King of Spain!' he shouted as the arrow shot away.

But when he picked out the third arrow it was the very one which had split the peg, it seemed ages ago – before the beacons were lit to signal England's danger.

Dick fitted that special arrow to the bow, then drawing it back so that the bow was bent to its limit, he aimed the arrow high over the cliff edge to the sea beyond. As the arrow flew, high and fast, Dick said, proudly:

'And that one is for the Spanish Armada!'

2 The Inside Story

Only six lifetimes ago, in the days of Queen Elizabeth the First, the world outside Europe 'belonged' to Spain and Portugal. The Pope in Rome declared this to be so and all other countries were warned to keep out. They were not allowed to visit the East Indies, America, India or the Spice Islands; and certainly not to trade there.

It was, of course, absurd to expect such a law to be obeyed and as everybody who has read about Sir Francis Drake will know, England paid no attention at all.

Drake captured Spanish galleons returning from the West full of treasure; he attacked Spanish towns in the West Indies and to show how little importance he placed upon the Pope's laws, he sailed right round the world in the famous *Golden Hind* and stopped to trade wherever he felt inclined.

King Philip of Spain became King of Portugal as well in 1580 which made him the richest and most powerful ruler in the world. He was furious with Drake and even angrier with Queen Elizabeth for letting him behave like a pirate – the Queen told Philip how sorry she was for the things he had done, then made Drake a knight! – and the King decided upon war. He collected together the Armada fleet and everybody said:

'Philip will soon be King of England as well. For how can little England possibly stand up against the most powerful country in the world?'

Yet a Spanish fleet of nearly 130 ships and an army of 60,000 soldiers were defeated. King Philip's great army could not invade England and of the great Armada fleet, only 80 ships managed to limp back to their home ports in Spain. The rest were lost around the British Isles.

In the story, you read what it was like to be in England at that exciting time. Now we come to the Inside Story of how the famous victory was won.

THE SPANISH PLAN

On board the 130 ships of the Spanish fleet there were far more soldiers than sailors. There were nearly 19,000 soldiers and only 10,000 sailors. This was because 'Armada' is Spanish for 'army' and, it was an army and not a navy that Philip sent to England. The ships were loaded with all the things needed for fighting a battle on land. Horses and mules, carts for carrying stores, materials for building bridges and for digging trenches.

It was really a very simple plan. The Armada was to sail to England and clear the way for the Duke of Parma to land the main force of the invasion. This meant destroying the English navy so that they could not interfere with the rowing boats which were to take the Duke's army across the Dover Straits. When they were safely across, the soldiers on board the Armada ships would land and join in the battle.

The Spaniards at this time were very old-fashioned about fighting. They believed there was honour only in hand-to-hand fighting – sword-to-sword or pike-to-pike. Noblemen should fight noblemen and ordinary soldiers should fight other soldiers. They did not like the new way of fighting – with guns. With a gun, a mere peasant could kill a lord! And that was quite against the rules.

The Spanish way of fighting at sea was for their warships to sail alongside the enemy so that soldiers could leap aboard and fight hand-to-hand. The officers of each ship could then fight together with swords and the common soldiers could kill each other with pikes or bows and arrows – which was quite all right!

That was how the Spanish intended to fight their way through the English Channel. But Queen Elizabeth's navy had other ideas.

THE ENGLISH PLAN

The real danger to England was from the Spanish army which might come ashore and fight its way inland. Spanish soldiers were famous for their skill and bravery for they had been fighting wars almost continuously and were very experienced. England, on the other hand, had been at peace all through Elizabeth's reign and had no army at all. But the Armada had been expected for more than ten years and during that time a system of 'trained bands' had been started. Every county of England was ordered to select men for training as part-time soldiers and the government gave orders for supplies of gunpowder and weapons for them to use.

It was not a very good way of building a strong army because the men were all farm workers, craftsmen, clerks or servants and they could only be trained as soldiers in holiday times. Ten days training a year were ordered; four days beginning on Easter Monday, four beginning on Whit Monday and two days after harvest. The part-time soldiers were to be paid eight pence a day during their training.

The best amongst the men were taught to be musketeers but guns were quite new weapons and many men were frightened by the bang they made. Their shooting was very bad because they flinched when their guns went off! The rest of the trained bands were armed with pikes and bills; and a few were armed with bows and arrows.

The officers were mostly the local gentry like Adam Ashburnham in the story, who were given the rank of captain and expected to teach themselves how to lead their men to war. There were no army barracks, parade grounds, military camps

or other places needed by a modern army. The soldiers and
their officers were scattered all over the countryside of England
in isolated farms, villages and towns. If they were needed they
had to be called together and formed into companies under
their officers. First they had to collect their arms, mostly
stored in village churches in rooms over the porches, and get
into any uniform they might have been given. Then they had
to make their way, usually on foot, to the place where they
did their annual training.

It was a slow business, but by the time the Armada appeared
off the coast of Cornwall, every county in England was ready
with more than 2,000 trained men for the defence of England.
The next problem was how they were to be used.

THE BEACONS

The coastline from Bristol, round Land's End, along the south
coast and up to the Wash, is more than a thousand miles and
every part of it was within reach of the Armada and the ten
thousand highly trained soldiers on board. Along some stret-
ches there were high cliffs which would make a landing impossible and elsewhere there were swamps inland which would
make movement difficult if a landing was made. But there were
still hundreds of beaches, and harbours too, where the invasion
could start. The problem was how to collect those widely

scattered trained bands together and get them to the threatened place in time.

Exactly the same question faced Fighter Command before the famous Battle of Britain. Then, instead of widely dispersed soldiers, there were Spitfires and Hurricanes at airfields scattered all round southern England. The fighters at these air bases had to be collected into formations and sent to attack the enemy aircraft and shoot them down before they could cross the coast and drop their bombs.

It was done, as we all know, by 'radar'. This was a special kind of radio wave which could 'see' enemy aircraft at night and through cloud or fog. German bombers and fighters could even be 'seen' taking off from their airfields in France. Our fighters were told how high to fly and in what direction, in order to meet the enemy. By this means we were able to collect together the largest possible number of fighters and send them quickly to meet the threat.

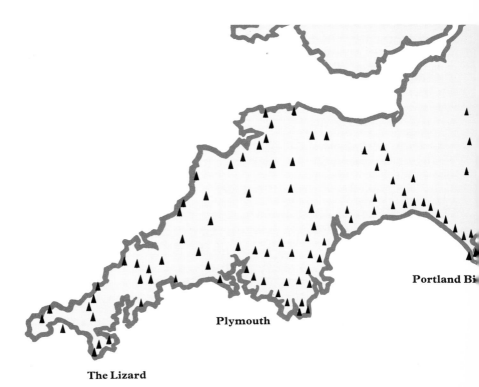

Portland Bi

Plymouth

The Lizard

The hilltop beacons you read about in the story were the radar stations of Elizabethan times. Their purpose was to make sure that if a Spanish army landed our trained bands could be collected together and marched quickly to the threatened place. The chart below shows the beacons along the south coast and some of the beacons which carried their warnings inland.

At the most important sites there were three beacons. One lit meant 'stand by'; two lit meant 'invasion likely – be ready to march'; three beacons burning meant 'landings here – come at once!' There were strict rules about lighting the beacons for enemy agents could have helped an invasion by lighting beacons in the wrong place. As you saw in the story, watchers were not allowed to light their beacons without permission from an officer – usually a local Justice of the Peace – and the watchmen were always armed so that they could defend their site in case agents did try to raise a false alarm.

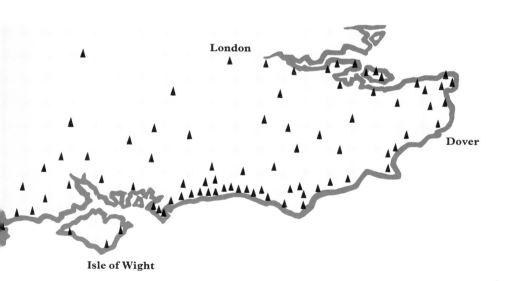

MAP OF THE SOUTH COAST BEACONS

Tar, like that used on roads – was burned in iron barrels to make the fire and on a clear day they could be seen from more than twenty miles away. If the weather was bad and the beacons could not be seen, horsemen were sent across country with the message. A watch was only kept during the summer months when an invasion was likely and then there were always two or three men on watch, day and night. It was not a very popular duty and it brought trouble to some watchmen. At Stanway beacon in Essex, two watchmen were severely punished when they were caught trapping partridges in a corn field when they should have been on watch. Two other watchers at Portsdown beacon behind Portsmouth got into trouble when they mistook smoke caused by huntsmen smoking out a badger for a beacon signal. They lit theirs and brought out the trained bands as far away as Berkshire! There is no record of what punishment they got.

THE NAVY
In 1940, we were fortunate in having Spitfire and Hurricane

fighters for the Battle of Britain. They were faster and more heavily armed than German fighters and in a straight fight could usually shoot them down. In 1588 we were just as fortunate in having warships which were faster and better armed than the Armada. This was due to John Hawkins who was Secretary of the Queen's navy and responsible for ordering and fitting out all new ships. He did away with the tall 'castles' at each end of the older ships (the front end of a modern ship is still called the 'forecastle' even though Hawkins did away with them four hundred years ago!) and he made his new ships longer and more streamlined. Then he armed them with the best guns he could buy.

Sir Francis Drake was the most experienced sailor in the Navy and he now decided how these fine new ships should be used against the Armada. King Henry the Eighth, more than thirty years earlier had invented the 'broadside' which meant firing off all the guns along one side of a warship at one time, but even that idea was only in order to blow down the masts and sails of an enemy ship so that she could be boarded and captured. Drake now decied that the broadside should be used instead actually to *sink* an enemy ship so that there would be no need to put men aboard. John Hawkins had fitted the ships out with guns which could fire iron or stone cannon balls weighing forty pounds for a distance of a mile or more. Drake's plan was to keep well away from the Armada ships so that they would have no chance of carrying out their usual plan of coming alongside and boarding. Then the English ships would bombard the Armada from a distance and sink their ships, one by one. Those were the plans of the two sides in the fight that was to come. Now we can see how, in practice, those plans worked out.

WHAT REALLY HAPPENED

The Armada was first sighted on Friday, 19th July. Captain Thomas Flemyng who had been at sea for several days watching the western approaches, sailed into Plymouth harbour in the late evening of that same day with the news. As everybody knows, he found the English captains playing bowls on Plymouth Hoe, and Francis Drake, hearing the news, merely said: 'We have time to finish the game and beat the Spaniards too . . .' then calmly went on with his bowls. Some people think that it was just a story to make Drake seem even more of a hero. But it was probably quite true because there really was plenty of time.

Winds blow mostly along the English Channel from west to east. That is the prevailing wind. The easiest voyage for a sailing ship therefore was eastwards, the way the Armada was sailing at that very time. When the wind was from the west it was difficult for a sailing ship to go westward; it was especially difficult for a fleet of ships, for they would have to 'tack' across the wind and for large numbers of ships close together this meant danger of collision.

Francis Drake therefore knew that if his fleet was to attack the Armada he would have to position them upwind of the Spaniards. From there he would be able to chase them down channel, firing his guns at them as they went. In other words, the best time to leave Plymouth harbour would be when the Armada was in sight, and according to Thomas Flemyng, they

were still quite a long way off. The tide, moreover, was flowing into Plymouth harbour – Thomas Flemyng's ship had been helped in by it – and it would not turn until midnight. That was the time for the English fleet to sail. So Drake really did have time to finish his game.

There was plenty of activity in the harbour all that evening nevertheless, for there were more than a hundred ships, 62 of them warships, which had to be prepared for the fight. Despite the incoming tide, many of them were 'warped' out – towed by men in rowing boats – to the harbour entrance, and by dawn the next day they were all out and getting into position upwind.

It took the Armada two full days to sail from the Scilly Isles to Plymouth Sound. That is only 100 miles so their speed averaged just two miles per hour! It was now that the English fleet showed its superior speed. The Armada dropped anchor outside Plymouth that night, not realising that the English fleet had left harbour and was already on its way tacking to the west, moving into the position from which to attack – upwind!

As dawn broke on Sunday, 21st of July, lookouts in the Armada ships sighted the enemy, bearing down on them from the west.

For seven long days the Armada was followed along the English Channel by the English fleet. They never had a chance to grapple with the English ships for they were far too nimble, outsailing the lumbering Spanish galleons with ease. They followed Drake's plan, staying well away, firing their guns from a distance and never coming close enough for the Spanish ships to come alongside. The Spaniards kept their close formation and fired back in answer to the English guns.

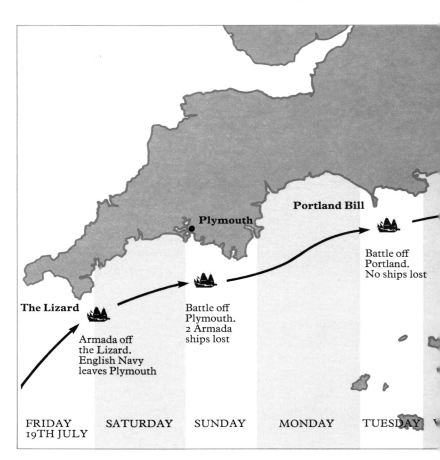

Portland Bill

Plymouth

Battle off
Portland.
No ships lost

The Lizard

Battle off
Plymouth.
2 Armada
ships lost

Armada off
the Lizard.
English Navy
leaves Plymouth

FRIDAY
19TH JULY   SATURDAY   SUNDAY   MONDAY   TUESDAY

But then the English ships found their plan going wrong. Their fine new guns had fired hundreds of cannon balls at the Spaniards – and had hit them. But not a single Armada ship had sunk. It was clear already that the cannon balls were not heavy enough to damage the galleons' hulls, let alone make holes large enough for them to sink. The Armada ships were too slow to catch the English fleet; the English guns were not heavy enough to sink the Spanish fleet. The fact was that neither fleet could harm the other!

If you study the chart you will see that several sea battles were fought – off Plymouth, Portland Bill, the Isle of Wight and Calais. But all that time, even though thousands of shots

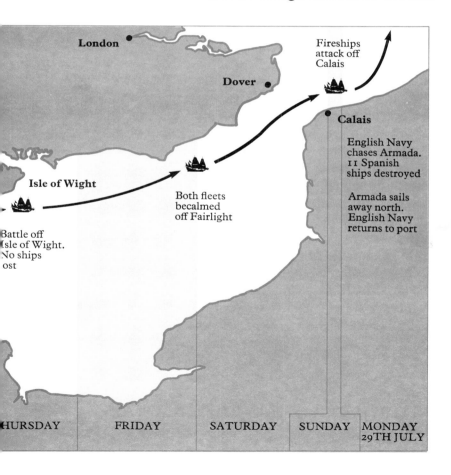

London

Dover

Fireships
attack off
Calais

Calais

Isle of Wight

Both fleets
becalmed
off Fairlight

English Navy
chases Armada.
11 Spanish
ships destroyed

Armada sails
away north.
English Navy
returns to port

Battle off
Isle of Wight.
No ships
lost

THURSDAY   FRIDAY   SATURDAY   SUNDAY   MONDAY
29TH JULY

were exchanged, the Armada kept its battle formation with the big warships surrounding the troop carriers and store ships to protect them, and hardly any damage was caused by either side.

It was not until the fireships were launched that the Armada lost formation and our ships were able to do real damage. Some Spanish ships were sunk and our new guns began to do the work expected of them. But then, our fleet *ran out of ammunition!* And so did the Armada!

All through the Channel fights, both fleets had been shooting at each other – except for that one day off Fairlight when they were both becalmed – and they had used all the ammunition on board. The Great Armada, expected to do so much, just fizzled out.

HOW IT ENDED

With no ammunition for their guns, there was only one thing left for the Armada to do – go home. It would have taken them several weeks to sail back through the English Channel against the prevailing wind. Even worse, the English fleet could send ashore for more ammunition. But there was no way for the Spaniards to get a new supply.

The only other way back to Spain was northwards, right round the top of Scotland; out beyond Ireland into the stormy Atlantic and south once more, past the Scilly Isles from where their unhappy adventure had begun. By now the Armada ships, many badly damaged in that last fierce battle before the ammunition ran out, were short of food and water. The men on board suffered terribly. Many of their ships were lost round the coast of Ireland and only eighty battered Spanish galleons eventually limped back to Spain.

The Duke of Parma, seeing no chance now for his troops to cross to England, marched them away, just as Napoleon Buonaparte did in 1805 and Adolf Hitler had to, in 1942. Not a single English ship was lost and less than 100 of our men were killed.

But they were exciting days. It must have been a grand sight, those two great fleets becalmed off Fairlight nearly four hundred years ago!

3 See Where it Happened

It is nearly 400 years since the great Spanish Armada set sail from Lisbon on its fateful journey up the English Channel. In that time the remains of the great galleons that were wrecked on the coasts of Scotland and Ireland have long since mouldered away. Divers have visited some of these wrecks and recovered bronze cannons, shot, anchors, and if they were lucky, gold and silver coins. Many of these objects are now on display in museums.

Although the ships have gone the treacherous coasts where they met their end are still there for all to see. So too are the hills where the beacons once blazed their warnings. On a clear day from the top of a 'beacon hill' it is fun to guess which of the hills within sight had the next beacon along the line. Often an Ordnance Survey map can help you to pick them out as many of the sites are still marked 'Beacon Hill' on the maps. As they were usually spaced six to eight miles apart there are hundreds of these beacon hills around the country. In the west country they are often called 'Fire beacon hill' which makes it even easier to identify them.

Here now is a selection of places which in one way or another preserve memories of those dangerous days nearly four centuries ago when the Spanish Armada set out to conquer England. Many of them are now looked after by the National Trust and they are marked like this *.

ENGLAND
CHESHIRE
Alderley Edge*
On the highest point of this hill a pile of stones marks the site of Alderley Beacon. It was used as a beacon site even before the time of the Armada. It is easy to see why when you look at the marvellous view from the top.

CORNWALL

Bass Point, Lizard Peninsula*

On 19 July 1588 the Armada fleet was visible from the Lizard as it moved slowly into the English Channel. From Bass Point on the southern tip of the peninsula you can get a fine view out to sea and along the coast.

Carne Beacon, nr Tregony*

The beacon is actually sited on a neolithic burial mound above Pendower beach.

St Agnes Beacon*

The beacon is 629 ft high and from the top you can see to the south coast and for twenty-six miles along the north coast.

St Michael's Mount*

Because of its prominent position in the bay, the beacon on the church tower of St Michael's Mount was one of the most important on the Cornish coast. It was one of the first to signal the approach of the Armada.

St. Michael's Mount

Drake's Drum

CO DURHAM
South Shields
In the main street near the sea there is an ancient sea anchor. It was recovered from the North Sea by a trawler in 1920 and there is a tradition that it came from one of the Armada ships on its terrible journey home.

DEVON
Bolt Tail, nr Salcombe*
The rocks under Bolt Tail are the watery grave of the '*San Pedro el Mayor*'. She was one of the two hospital ships which sailed with the Spanish fleet and was the only Armada ship wrecked on English coasts.
Buckland Abbey*
Sir Francis Drake bought Buckland Abbey from another famous sailor, Sir Richard Grenville, after his epic voyage around the world. It was here that he helped organise the defences of the Devon and Cornish coasts and planned the tactics that defeated the Armada. There are many memories of the great man here including his famous drum, a model of his ship the *Golden Hind,* and his accounts for equipping the English fleet against the Armada.

Compton Castle

Compton Castle*

During Elizabeth I's reign the castle was owned by the Gilbert family. They were related to Sir Walter Raleigh and the four Gilbert brothers were great seafarers and adventurers. They played an important part in the defence of Devon and later joined the expedition to found colonies in America. Sir John Gilbert was Sheriff of Devon in 1572 and later Vice-Admiral of Devon. This meant he was responsible for the beacons and the trained bands. Sir John sent his own ship, the *Gabriel* of 150 tons, to join the English fleet against the Armada, and one of his brothers did the same.

DORSET
Chilcombe
The little church at Chilcombe is one of the smallest in England. It has a carved screen which is said to have come from a captured galleon of the Armada fleet.
Thorncombe Beacon, nr Charmouth*
The hill is 508 ft high and was one of the chain of beacons on the cliff-tops of the south coast.

EAST SUSSEX
Ditchling Beacon*
This was an ancient hill-fort long before it became a beacon site.
Fairlight, nr Hastings*
This is the site of the beacon you read about in the story. It is now owned by the National Trust. It is impossible to know exactly where the beacon was situated but if you find the highest point on the down you can be sure it was nearby.

ESSEX
Lingwood Common, nr Chelmsford*
The highest point on the common is known as Beacon Hill.

HEREFORD AND WORCESTER
Herefordshire Beacon, nr Ledbury
This great Iron-Age fort on a hill over 1,000 ft high, was one of the major beacon sites in the country.

HERTFORDSHIRE
Ivinghoe Beacon, nr Berkhamsted*
The hill is 700 ft high and like many of the beacon sites is an ancient hill-fort.

LONDON
National Maritime Museum, Greenwich, SE10
This is one of the largest ship museums in the world and

contains many models and exhibits illustrating the Elizabethan Navy.

Tower of London
The White Tower contains a fine collection of arms and armour including weapons from the time of Queen Elizabeth I.

NORTH YORKSHIRE
Scarth Wood Moor, nr Northallerton*
On the highest point of the moor, overlooking Ancliffe Wood to the south-west, is the site of a beacon which has existed since the Middle Ages.

OXFORDSHIRE
Weston-on-the-Green
In the church there is an iron cross which is supposed to be from the masthead of an Armada ship.

SOMERSET
Holnicote Estate, Exmoor*
The National Trust land on Exmoor includes two of the most

Dunkery Beacon

Herefordshire Beacon

important beacon sites on the line which guarded the Bristol Channel. East of Porlock is Selworthy Beacon. South, at 1,705 ft the highest point on Exmoor, is Dunkery Beacon from which on a clear day six or seven counties can be seen.

WEST SUSSEX
Black Down, nr Haslemere*
At 918 ft this is the highest point in the county and was an obvious site for the Elizabethan beacon which used to stand here.
Glatting Beacon, nr Bognor Regis*
This was an important beacon site as there are views from it southward to the coast and northward to the Weald.

NORTHERN IRELAND
BELFAST
Ulster Museum
On display in the museum is the treasure salvaged by divers from the wreck of the *Girona*.

CO ANTRIM
Port-na-Spaniagh*
The North Antrim Cliff Path, owned by the National Trust, goes past Port-na-Spaniagh. In 1967 divers found the wreck

of the galleas *Girona* here. When she sank there were 1,300 men on board, many of whom had already survived two previous shipwrecks further down the coast. Only nine men survived from the *Girona* wreck. The treasure which the divers found is now on display in the Ulster Museum.

SCOTLAND
ISLE OF MULL
Tobermory
In Tobermory Bay lies the wreck of the galleon *San Juan de Sicilia*. The story goes that she anchored here to take on provisions for the voyage back to Spain. The ship was delayed because the captain, Don Diego Tellez Henriquez, hired out his men as soldiers to the local Scottish chieftain in return for provisions. When the English heard there was a Spanish galleon at Tobermory they sent a secret agent, John Smollett, to blow it up. He succeeded in getting on board and struck a match in the powder room just as the ship was getting under way. She blew up and sank at the entrance to the bay.

WALES
CLWYD
Llandrillo-yn-Rhos
On top of the church tower in the village is a small stone turret. It contains a recess for supporting the brazier for a fire beacon. It was one of a line of four beacons along the north coast of Wales.

MAP OF PLACES
MENTIONED IN CHAPTER 3
🦅 National Trust sites
𝒬 Other places of interest

𝒬 Tobermory

Port-na-Spaniagh
🦅

𝒬
Ulster
Museum

South 𝒬
Shields

Scarth
Wood 🦅
Moor

𝒬
Llandrillo-yn-Rhos

🦅 Alderley Edge

Herefordshire Beacon
𝒬

Ivinghoe
Beacon
🦅

Lingwood
Common
🦅

Weston 𝒬

The Tower 𝒬
𝒬
Greenwich

Black
Down 🦅

Fairlight
🦅

Holnicote Estate
🦅

Glatting Beacon 🦅
🦅
Ditchling
Beacon

Thorncombe
Beacon 🦅
𝒬

Buckland
Abbey
🦅

St Agnes
Beacon
🦅

Carne
Beacon

Compton
Castle 🦅

Chilcombe 𝒬

Bolt Tail
🦅

Michael's 🦅
Mount

Bass
Point